AMERICA
From Sea to Shining Sea

Wallace Kirkland

Published by
HOME LIBRARY PUBLISHING COMPANY
Fort Atkinson, Wisconsin

Ray Atkeson

The Editors are grateful to the following publishers for permission to include the following copyrighted material in this volume: Random House, Inc., for the prologue to *Big Woods* by William Faulkner; copyright 1951 by William Faulkner; reprinted by permission of Random House, Inc.
Houghton Mifflin Company for excerpt from *Across the Wide Missouri* by Bernard De Voto.

CONTENTS

The shores of Cape Hatteras, North Carolina.

The moth mullein's two- to six-foot-tall
stalks flower in dry Western ranges.

I
GEOGRAPHY
OF HOPE

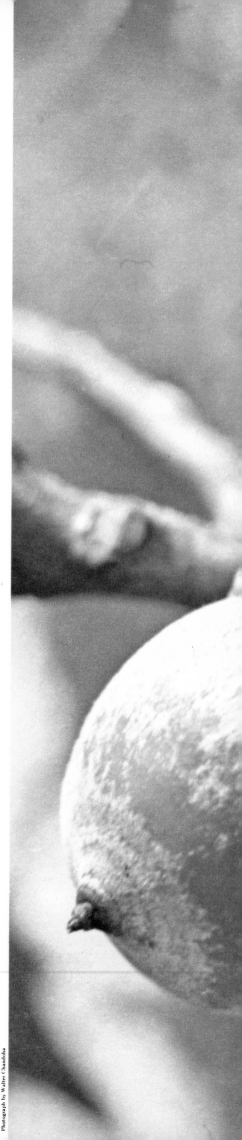

From the subtle strength of a seed to the wild freedom of a flower, nature displays the perfections and abundance that could be a part of every American. Giving each its role, dignity, and value to the next, nature lives what discordant citizens seek. What men can now see, hear, and touch of nature has become a key to understanding and preserving themselves.

THE OAK'S LONGEVITY

The oak is a tree of great longevity: The same oaks which the Saxons saw in England some nine hundred years ago still stand today. These sturdy trees are known, too, for their solid, heavy wood: Railroads used the wood of the numerous oaks of North America for ties that carried rails across a continent; cabinetmakers labored hard over oak boards with the knowledge that the extra effort needed to fashion such hardwood resulted in highly prized, well-constructed, lasting furniture.

The oak's seed, or fruit, is the acorn, more usually seen by man in the fall after it has turned a nutty brown and has dropped to the ground; yet, in summer, the acorn, still green, has already become full and rich. Like the tree from which it comes, the acorn is robust and enduring; it is not easily stifled in its course of growing eventually into a great tree. In the acorn then, there is strength devoted to re-creation, and in such strength there is true nobility.

Robust and enduring, green acorns harbor the promise of a great tree.

Photograph by Walter Chandoha

A pine forest where nature orders night and day, season and year, century and eon.

THE STILLNESS OF PINES

Any pine forest is more than a woodland. It is a summary of time and place and change, of eternal matters of the earth and the universe. There is little haste in a tree; the clock of the tree ticks off only night and day, season and year, century and eon. . . .

I cross the wall and am in the pine woods. Fifty yards and I am in the midst of the stillness. Not silence, but stillness. A stillness composed of natural sounds: a breeze in the treetops, a distant cry of a blue jay, the murmur of a brook a hundred yards away, the echoing rattle of a pileated woodpecker announcing himself on a dead branch. Muted sounds, somehow, muted by the pines themselves.

If I listened closely I might hear my own pulse, or some great rhythm of which it is a part. I know I can hear my own thoughts. And I think of the man who once came to these woods with me and stood for a long minute, eyes closed, then whispered, "I heard an acorn fall!" I smiled. It made no difference that acorns grow on oaks, not pines. He had heard something that to him was an acorn falling, and it was a miracle. He wasn't talking about acorns; he was talking about himself.

The brook is a hundred yards away. It comes from beyond the pines on up the mountainside, from a seep spring among the rocks. It chatters down to the pines, then eases to a quiet flow as though hushed by the trees. It flows leisurely through the woods, widening into clear, shallow pools. . . .

Overhead is the distant drone of an airplane, man a-wing, triumphant in the air, but tied to the earth by the air itself. Far off, over the hills on the highway, is the hum and faint roar of traffic, man a-wheel, triumphant in his conquest of distance. Hurrying, hurrying, to the tick of a clock. And behind me is the pine woods, which has no boast, no urgency, no clamor of importance, but only the truth of a seed, which is fundamental. The truth of the earth, of the universe, of life. . . .

Before I seat myself at my desk I pause and look out the window that faces the mountain and the pine woods. We have renewed our acquaintance at first hand, and I have somewhat renewed my understanding of myself.

HAL BORLAND

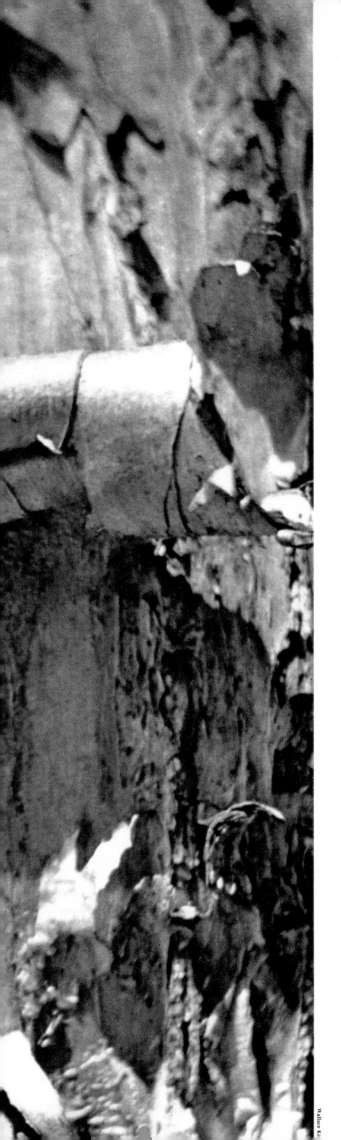

Wallace K...

OLD BARK

Ancient Latins used a tree's inner bark to write on. . . . American Indians wrote their sign language upon the clean bark of the white birch tree and also used bark for canoes, utensils and the roofs of wigwams. Thus bark is functional and important for man as well as tree. But perhaps the greatest contribution it has to offer man today is the look of it: Gnarled, split apart, curling into tight little rolls — the bark of a fine tree can remind us that, although time passes for man and tree alike, such a hazard can be borne with an admirable persistence.

Gnarled, split, curled bark of a fine birch that has borne time with admirable persistence.

Wisconsin pond: Throughout the country 1.5 million such natural reservoirs conserve two million acres of water.

THE POND

Beneath the lily pads, above the water, along the shore flourishes a "city" in the wilderness, where each inhabitant lives beside others. In and around the pond, each form of life has its occupation. Even microscopic bacteria have great purpose; they feed upon wastes to decompose them before the wastes pile high and engulf all other creatures. And, the habits of the crustaceans and amphibians demonstrate the way the work of the pond ties to the work of the land. The crayfish is the necessary scavenger.

The frog feeds on insects and, as he grows older, he tends to move away and reside on the land, carrying away the organic matter of the pond. Both, of course, may themselves become the food for animals of either the land or the water.

The summer vacationer in planning his two weeks at a lake resort is careful not to pick one on a marshy shore, where cattails, lily pads and bulrushes will foul his trolling lines and prevent his children from swimming. Yet, if it were not for these "weeds," the life of the lake could not exist. The rooted plants contribute needed oxygen to the water and consume its carbon

dioxide; they afford shelter for creatures in the breeding stage so they will not be destroyed.

While the muskrat seems to belong at the pond (he eats mainly grasses and stems of cattails), the raccoon is thought by some to be an interloper, a clever swimmer who preys upon fish life, removing it from the pond. In truth, though, there are no interlopers here; the raccoon, in eating the fish, later enriches the land surrounding the pond. As a predator, he serves other, more complex needs, even those of his prey. If this pond had no inhabitant such as the raccoon, others, like the fish which thrives on

The muskrat, largely vegetarian, will soon be joined by young tadpoles in balancing the pond's plant growth.

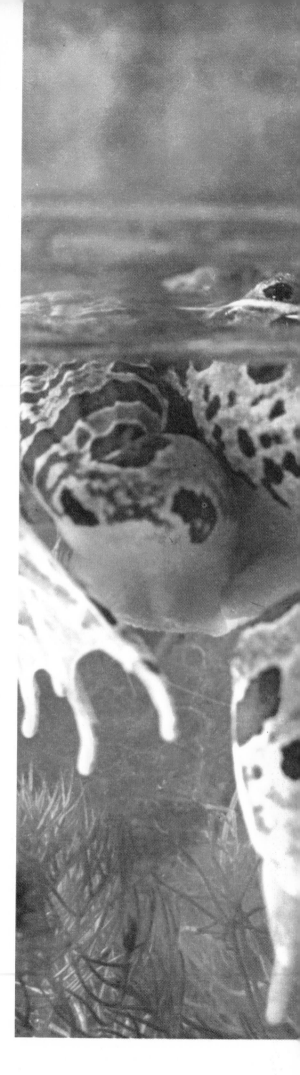

plant life, might reproduce in such numbers that all the available food could become exhausted. Thus the life of the pond requires, first of all, a coming-together of all sorts of life. An equilibrium results, the pond flourishes and this balance is upset only by some gigantic outside force, like man with his ravaging bulldozer or his sewage. . . .

Early visitors to America have told of the enchantment they felt in tramping through the wilderness. They told of hearing a thousand voices and, at first, not knowing their origin. Finally, after investigation, they learned the voices came from nearby ponds and marshes. There, they found the "concert hall" of the American wilderness. From its stage came the calls of the frogs — calls so varied in style that in later years they would be recorded and heard in the nation's living rooms. Also, from the grasses of the pond littorals came the songs of the gallinules, rails, coots and other marsh birds, including the famed, easy-to-recognize red-wing blackbirds. Today, as man pushes out the suburbs, he can again hear the concerts of nearby ponds, unless, of course, the television set, automobile, power mower and jet plane drown them out.

SIMPLE PERFECTION

The charms and terrors of the sea have impressed man for thousands of years, but most of these experiences are available only to those who regularly or occasionally journey across oceans or the largest lakes. Fortunately, one part of the sea where many of its most curious offerings can be found is also accessible to the landlubber — the tidal pools which lie along beaches and rocky shores.

Here abundant plant and animal life dwells in a great diversity of shape and color. Among the inhabitants to be seen is a five-legged echinoderm commonly called the starfish. Neither the simplest nor the most advanced of creatures, it nevertheless has a perfection all its own, especially when viewed in its natural habitat.

The simple perfections of a starfish delight the explorer of our coastal tidal pools.

Weston from Rapho-Guillumette

A young boy wanders over the dunes with the primordial urge to return to the land beside the sea.

RETURN TO THE SEASHORE   Somewhere, a young boy who feels the primordial urge to return to the land beside the sea will wander over a stretch of dunes, kicking his feet through the sand long before it is warm enough to sunbathe or swim or build castles in the sand.

United States Department of the Interior.
National Park Service Photo by W. Woodbridge Williams

DRUID ARCH

There is one view that perhaps readers have never heard of or seen, a view tucked away in a fantastic region of eroded sandstone in southeastern Utah. The place is the canyonlands area now being proposed as a national park; the feature is Druid Arch.

Druid Arch is aptly named. Towering like the great Stonehenge where the ancient Druids paid homage to their gods, this landmark, created by wind and water, stood for centuries before it was first seen by white men only a few years ago, initially from the air and later confirmed by a party on foot.

Nothing about the Arch is easy: Getting there is a rugged walk over a primitive trail (requiring ropes at two points along the way); and trying to describe it afterward is even more difficult. Although viewed to date by only a handful of hardy hikers, it is, in my opinion, a sight of rare beauty. The miles and miles of fantastically eroded wilderness surrounding it preclude the possibility of it ever being casually accessible, and herein lies its real beauty. In today's world there are few such places where man must put aside his awesome machines and technology and, in a sense, be on his own. As author Wallace Stegner said, ". . . It can be a means of reassuring ourselves of our sanity as creatures, a part of the geography of hope."

STEWART L. UDALL

Druid Arch, a monument of eroded sandstone, highlights the canyonlands of southeastern Utah.

SHEEPHERDERS OF THE WEST

The sheepherder must see all his herd, fanned out and on good graze, and yonder is good water. He must see that ewes don't stray too far, that frolic lambs don't gambol up a draw and disappear. We ask ourselves, those of us not herders, what manner of men these are. What manner, to sit and look the long day through? To talk to self as herders do? To watch the empty distances? To see the far line of the skyline and the vacant land between and feel that here is life?

The herder is convivial, open-handed, and easy, but he doesn't belong in town. He belongs to himself and to the open, obligated only to the dog that is his closest friend. Sheepherders of the West live in solitude, die in devotion to duty, and wear a look of distance on their faces. . . .

The herder has sat solitary all day, looking not at sheep alone but at the biggest country we in America can ever know. Distance streams away, to the up-lip of the horizon that is the eye's reach. That butte, now, that ridge, a hundred miles beyond, blue against the deep blue of the skyline, yet there they are. And that mountain — how high does it climb? The herder sees, though he may not understand, time against eternity, now to everlasting.

A. B. GUTHRIE, JR.

The Western sheepherder and his flock wander through America's untrammeled countryside.

Winter completes the year and makes our land whole again.

THE MYSTERY OF WINTER

Maybe one doesn't have to live in the country to appreciate winter, but it helps. Winter has many dimensions, and unless one can stand on a hilltop or walk up a valley stripped to simple fundamentals, one misses some of them. Winter is more than a season bounded by a solstice and an equinox, more even than snowstorms and icebound rivers and winds whooping down from the frozen arctic tundra. It is primitive forces at work, cleansing and scarifying the earth, but it is also beautiful and awesome and full of wonder. It rounds out the year, makes it whole; and, in human terms, it takes the edge off human arrogance at the same time that it makes the countryman proud of his own competence. In a sense, it makes the man who lives with winter whole again, too.

The world is wider than a cornfield or a city block, and the sky is higher than a silo or a skyscraper, and a man needs a time and he needs a place to realize it. A man needs a winter hilltop. . . .

No one can live close to the soil and refuse to participate. First principles are involved, and you ignore them at your peril. If you would be warm and fed in winter, you must know the summer's sweat and muscle-ache. The truth of cause and effect is written across every day and every hilltop. You are a part of this world; your blood is a freight of hemoglobin in a stream of

Photograph by Robert Holland

ocean brine, and the hemoglobin is only an atom or two removed from the green chlorophyll in a leaf. Your pulse is as insistent as the rhythm of the days and the seasons. You are of the earth and the universe. You can't resign. You know that you are more than an integer in the census statistics, more than a dot on a population chart. You are a sentient human being still capable of wonder.

I sometimes think, on a winter evening, that winter was patterned into the year not only to give the earth a time of rest but to urge man to catch his breath and accept this world, whole and round and complete. Winter is completion, the inevitable complement of summer. When I look out upon the world after the first snowfall I always think that it is brand new, another kind of genesis, innocent and waiting for new and better transcriptions. Not only is the clutter and litter of autumn hidden and simplified, but the whole scene of man's argument and confusion is cleansed and made briefly immaculate. All things are possible again. Even wisdom. Even understanding.

Yet I know that winter is both change and time, time forever flowing. It is yesterday maturing into tomorrow. Even the autumn debris in the woodland which winter clothes and simplifies is the latent humus in which tomorrow's trees must sprout and grow. Winter is the dormant bud upon the bough, the berry committed to the waiting seed, the insect in the fertile egg. It is the fundamental miracle of the year, another cycle in the eternal rhythm of which we all partake.

HAL BORLAND

SANCTUARIES of NATURE

The ages had been at work on the land long before the breed called Americans came to claim it — and a majestic legacy remains.

Magnolia-on-the-Ashley combines the strange beauty of cypress swamps with aged oaks and lawns, brilliant azaleas, camellias and rhododendrons. The famed gardens began over one hundred years ago as the modest project of Reverend Grimke-Drayton and flowered into an incomparable vision.

Magnolia Gardens, Charleston, South Carolina. (Dick Smith)

Hot springs and geysers maintain water warm enough for the trumpeter swan to remain in the park year around. Yellowstone is one refuge for this species whose numbers have become precariously few in the last decade.

Trumpeter swans, Yellowstone National Park, Wyoming, Idaho and Montana. (David Muench)

The geological history of the Rocky Mountains started over a billion years ago with the sedimentary layers of a prehistoric sea. Time, pressure and chemical changes solidified the layers until they emerged from under immense glaciers 60 million years ago. The area warmed to its present subarctic climate which supports alpine flora and hardy wildlife among the remaining ice-rivers.

Glacier lilies, Logan Pass, Glacier National Park, Montana. (David Muench)

The Green and the Colorado rivers meet in Canyonlands to form a land laced with tangles of gorges, narrow roads, dust-dry creek beds and sagebrush. From this point the features of desert, plateau, arroyos, embayments and basins are visible. Other sections of this sandstone land retain marks of departed Indians and of prehistoric men and animals.

Grandview Point, Canyonlands National Park, Utah. (David Muench)

29

"Grand" seems an understatement of the Colorado River's famous canyon: The water-wrought stone sculpture is 217 miles long, averages a mile deep and spreads nine miles across in panorama. Before John Westley Powell was enticed to lead an expedition through in 1869, for three thousand years the canyon's splendor had drawn trappers, conquistadors and, before them, primitive hunters.

Prickly pear blossoms, South Rim, Grand Canyon National Park, Arizona. (David Muench)

Only in Hawaii do the states touch the Orient. The ancient Hawaiian name for this garden place was *Pa 'u-a-Laka,* or the "Skirt of Laka," the goddess of the hula whose temple was here. The sensuality that her name evokes harmonizes with the unusual beauty of the tropic plants. Their succulence and vivid colors are rarely matched in mainland varieties of cacti, aloes and orchids.

Cacti and tropical water lilies, Plantation Garden (Moir's), Koloa, Kauai, Hawaii. (Bud Carter)

II
FRONTIERS OF FREEDOM

America lives by the lives of its people. Look to the land and the sea, the farms, towns, and cities. Search for the ideals which forged our nation and the spirit that enlivens our heritage today. Reach into the lives of our countrymen and touch the truths of our tomorrow.

George Washington receives the Constitution from James Madison. Mural by Barry Faulkner, National Archives, Washington, D.C.

THE AMERICAN IDEA

John Adams, Franklin, Washington, Jefferson, and others agreed upon certain principles that, bound together, gave us most of the American Idea. These men fought for three principles that were an outgrowth of Western civilization, and that, in combination, stand related to the Christian spirit: the principles of liberty, equality, and toleration. Their roots can be traced back into Greek and Hebraic civilization, but their *true* development began under the benign influence of Christianity.

The basic doctrine of Christianity was distinguished by its emphasis on the brotherhood of man, which means equality before God; its emphasis on the law of love, which includes toleration; and its emphasis on the importance of the inward life, which means that while the Christian recognized the claims of the state, he insisted on the value of the individual and his right to full self-development. . . .

The four most representative leaders of the general revolution of the time — Franklin, Washington, Hamilton, and Jefferson — were men of character as well as intellectual power. Standing first among them, as men granted at that time as well as later, was Washington. Without his force of character, the struggle would have been lost. All the hope of lifting America from a group of weak and fettered colonies to the position of the most influential republic yet born rested upon his courage, patient endurance, elevation of spirit, devotion to the public good without selfish taint, and general balance of traits — just the right sternness, the right magnanimity, the right energy in immediate action, and the right wisdom for the future. For once, it seems, history had an Indispensable Man.

Franklin, who educated himself in letters and morality, had a marked capacity for expressing the three principles pithily:

Those who would give up essential liberty to purchase a little temporary safety deserve neither liberty nor safety — so much for freedom.

A plowman on his legs is higher than a nobleman on his knees — so much for equality.

Mix not in debate, with bigots in religion or the state — so much for toleration.

In the struggle for independence, Franklin played as important a role as anybody. He was not only foremost in the cause of liberty, but he had one distinction that our three other heroes could not share: He saw that American liberty could be a beacon to the entire globe, inspiring envy and imitation in lands that lacked it.

"All Europe is on our side of the question," he wrote an American friend from Paris in 1777. "Those who live under arbitrary power do nevertheless approve of liberty, and wish for it; they almost despair of recovering it in Europe; they read the translations of our separate constitutions with rapture; and there are such numbers everywhere who talk of removing to America, with their families and fortunes, as peace and our independence are established, that it is generally believed that we shall have a prodigious addition of strength, wealth, and arts."

Franklin detested gross inequalities of wealth. Most governments, he asserted, paid too much deference to property. Created by society, property "is subject to the calls of that society, whenever its necessities shall require it, even to the last farthing" — a doctrine with an advanced social flavor. He favored universal male suffrage, abolition of test oaths and other impediments, and perfect equality of representation — all accepted today as part of the American Idea.

Though he was himself a Deist, he aided various different sects in building churches, for he held that government and society need the support of religious faith.

As befitted a believer in equality, Franklin always abominated slavery, and in his last days became president of an abolitionist society. And, as befitted an adherent of toleration, he approved of the great victory won for religious freedom in Virginia. . . .

Believing in much the same grand objects, the founding fathers favored quite different modes of attaining them, but these modes, when fitted together, made a harmonious whole. Jefferson wished to give men a *larger* freedom by offering the individual a wide, unfenced field in which to move. Hamilton desired to give men a surer freedom by making the field efficient in government and organization. Jefferson wished to *safeguard* the equality of men by legal prohibitions of any encroachment on their privileges. Hamilton desired to *promote* the equality of men by encouraging economic forces — manufacturing, sound finance, stable economic enterprise — that would lift the standard of well-being for all.

Jefferson said: "Reason and free inquiry are the only effectual agents against error. It is error alone which needs the support of government. Truth can stand by itself." . . . "Every government degenerates when trusted to the rulers of the people alone. The people themselves are therefore its only safe repositories."

Yet, in a real sense, Hamilton has had the clearer victory. If Jefferson rules the spirit of men, Hamilton rules their lives. The growth of the nation has conformed more largely to the principles he laid down for its practical concerns. He, too, wanted liberty, but he believed that anarchy, party rancor, or idle drift would be deadlier enemies to it than authority. He stood for equality before the law, but he felt sure that men in the mass could never govern the state so well as select groups of successful men. Admitting that the people are the legitimate fountain of power, he maintained that their reason, not their passions, must be called forth.

As Jefferson was indispensable for the spiritual growth of the nation, Hamilton was indispensable for its material development. One looked to the soul, the other to the body. Between them, they completed for future growth the American Idea.

Happy is the country that has four such men in the morning of its history! That they appeared when the moment was ripe — and that they called forth so potent a body of popular support — must always be one of the most marvelous facts in our national career.

ALLAN NEVINS

Middleton Place near Charleston, South Carolina, was the home of Henry Middleton, President of the First Continental Congress, and his son, Arthur, a signer of the Declaration of Independence.

LIFE IN THE APPALACHIANS

These crested Appalachians, are home for four million people. It is a proud land; we are a proud people. It is a rugged and individualistic and loving land; so are the people.

Contrary to suppositions that the Southern Appalachians were settled by outlaws and renegades, the early western movement was dominated by the most patriotic, fierce-fighting, physically-fit pioneers of the Atlantic tidewater. Two decades before the Revolutionary War, these sons and daughters of earlier pioneers, who first shoved the Indians and the forests westward, began pressing further inland from the Virginia and North Carolina coastland.

They ascended the high mountains. They trekked up the valleys and through the passes and over the crests — and settled one of the most inaccessible parts of America. Usually a group of families went together, and each had its Bible whether one in the family could read or not.

The Southern Appalachians, home of determined, defiant, industrious, and independent pioneers.

Thomas K. Ber

And they also brought their musical instruments: guitars, fiddles, banjos, mandolins, and dulcimers.

Resourcefulness was their stock in trade; to survive, they *had* to have something above their ears and their elbows. The men were seasoned Indian fighters, experts with rifle and axe. They feared God and hated the Devil, the Indians, and the British.

Most of the able-bodied men bore arms in the Continental Army during the American Revolution. The others stayed home to fight attacking Indians from the Northwest Territory who, instigated by the British, were burning fortresses, homes, and people with equal in-discrimination.

The massacres were countless, lost now in the tumult of history. But these pioneers, determined and defiant, industrious and independent, persevered and eventually prevailed — and left their characteristics as a rich heritage to their modern descendents.

Our land is our livelihood. Our land is our life. Our small farms that we own and love, farms our fathers and fathers' fathers farmed before us, have made us free men. And one free man, after some of my observations, is worth thirty *yes men* who bow to despotism. In all of America, no segment of the people like private ownership more than the highlanders. We are believers in freedom and will fight for it. We have received much criticism for our acts against what we think is unfairness, but, after just having visited fifteen countries in Africa, the Near East, and Europe, I am convinced that we should be proud of our individualism, our fierce love of freedom, our original culture within a country's culture.

JESSE STUART

Above: Independence and rugged resourcefulness closely unite highland generations on their modest farms.

Below: Making molasses, the Kentucky highlander derives joy from being close to the living land.

Dick Vennerbeck from Shostal

Julius Fanta from Shostal

MEN OF THE COAST

The ways of the coast are never old and never up-to-date. Required of the fisherman, now as always, is an adjustment amounting to dedication — his reason, his wit, his skill and endurance, his nature, are incessantly trained and tested by the challenges of a profession that must be followed in a region of eternal conflict.

The sea and the coast are a border region of forces never reconciled and never tamed. Some say they are a heritage to which men are born and bred. . . .

By and large through the years, those who have followed the calling of the banks and the coast have done so because they preferred it. They complain, they undergo ordeals, they sometimes decide that day labor ashore is better than work afloat, but the fishermen are an emancipated lot. In the discipline of the sea there is also much freedom, along with self-reliance. The labor is done in good company, and the good company persists after the labor is ended — until the next time. Fishermen traditionally work not for hire but on shares; they get what they can earn, and they have a rare feeling that it is good, fresh, clean money.

HENRY BEETLE HOUGH

Above left: Typical of the New England fisherman is the network of fine lines about the eyes.

Above right: New England fishermen thrive on silences born of violent winds and waters, hard work and close friends.

*Winston Churchill said,
"We shape our
buildings and afterward
our buildings shape us."
Public buildings from
America's past and
the dwellings of her
heroes reveal the
varied ideals and
activities of our people.*

BUILDINGS from AMERICA'S PAST

Colonial Williamsburg is a close recon-
struction of the original town and the
first large scale historic restoration
in the country. In the capitol building
in 1765, Patrick Henry first spoke
against the Stamp Act; the resolution
to begin the Committees of Correspondence
was adopted in 1773; and in May 1776, the
Virginia convention asked Congress to
declare the colonies independent states.

Colonial Williamsburg Capitol, Virginia. (Courtesy
Colonial Williamsburg)

A classic of Greek Revival style, the
mansion overlooks the historic and
beautiful Arlington National Cemetery in
Virginia, across the Potomac from Washington,
D.C. Robert E. Lee and his wife — Mary
Custis, foster great-granddaughter of
George Washington — lived here until the
outbreak of the Civil War, when Lee left to
assume command of the Army of the Confederacy.

Custis-Lee Mansion, Arlington, Virginia. (FPG by
Anderson)

The palace is an early prototype of a truely American architectural form—the combination of Indian and Spanish design. Built in 1610 by Don Pedro de Peralta, it is the oldest surviving public building in the continental states. Once it was the capital of a seventeenth-century Spanish province bounded only by the Pacific and the Mississippi, with no northern border.

Palace of the Governors, Santa Fe, New Mexico. (Harvey Caplin)

In the old Pennsylvania State House, venerated as "Independence Hall," both the Declaration of Independence and the United States Constitution were signed. For occasional periods during the Revolution the building also served as the national capitol.

Independence Hall, Philadelphia, Pennsylvania

In 1619, the first representative assembly in America—the House of Burgesses—met on this site in the Argall Church. Presently the ruins of the tower of the fifth church in Jamestown, a reminder of the earlier colonial sanctuaries here, are joined to the Episcopal memorial church.

Episcopal Church, Jamestown, Virginia. (Courtesy the Virginia Department of Conservation and Economic Development, Dementi Studio)

III
NOT IN ANGER, NOT IN FEAR

Some famous, some unknown, some individuals dared to be different. Different from the current thought and group pressure, they lived to change a town or a talent to better our nation. Not looking back in anger, nor forward in fear, they lived in the awareness of what they made of America, America would make of its men.

BOSTON'S NORTH END NEIGHBORHOOD

Many Bostonians would be glad to see the North End disappear. Knowing it only through quick visits to its historic buildings, they regard it as a regrettable pocket of slum. In reality, it is one of the few remaining communities in a large American city that manifests the values we claim to believe in. . . .

Those planners across the nation who deplore neighborhoods like the North End, considering them blighted, have failed to create housing projects, apartments and suburban developments that can boast what the North End takes for granted — a true sense of community and an exciting daily life. A neighborhood is a natural, self-creating organism; it comes into existence when people feel deep, spontaneous loyalty to their homes, their neighbors and the little local scenes and events that form the pattern of their daily life.

In spite of its poverty for a long time, the North End has been a true neighborhood for three hundred years. The English who lived there first must have thought the influx of Irish meant the end of the North End. As the euphemism says, the neighborhood was changing. But it still remained a neighborhood in the deepest sense — people living together and liking it. It was a neighborhood for the Jews and Italians who followed, and it is that for the new student and artist community moving in now.

Street markets help to give Boston's 300-year-old North End a true sense of community.

Photograph by Ted Polumbaum—Pix

What matters is not that a neighborhood changes, but that it keeps the subtle complex of personal and communal relationships that give it the necessary cohesion and vitality.

Plans to rehabilitate the North End rather than destroy it seem almost sure of approval now. It has been realized at last that were it replaced by bigger and better traffic arteries, supermarkets and middle-income pueblos, it would be one more step toward the destruction of the true American legend — that in which people from other countries added their riches to our diverse, eclectic nation and built here a home they called their own.

ARNO KARLEN

45

PRIVATE FORTUNES AND PUBLIC WEALTH

"Great private fortunes are simply reservoirs of public wealth," Henry Ford once said. This statement is subject to some reservations. Very rich men usually manage to keep part of their wealth in the family line. But it is essentially true, as Henry and Edsel Ford demonstrated when they placed nearly all their accumulations in the Ford Foundation. The man who gave the first spectacular proof of the wisdom of public use of private fortunes was Andrew Carnegie; and in doing it he moderated the attitude of Americans toward great holdings. . . .

The circumstances of his rise from poverty might easily have made him a hard, griping money-maker; but family standards and innate character gave him a different bent. He remained sunny, generous, and extroverted; anxious to make and save money, but also to be friendly and useful.

For his place among American industrialists Carnegie will be long remembered; but he should still longer be recalled for the transformation he wrought in the public attitude toward great wealth and concentrated economic power.

Carnegie published his famous article of 1889 in the *North American Review* on "The Disgrace of Dying Rich." In this he not only declared that large fortunes should be given away; he said they should be given away *intelligently*. "Of every thousand dollars spent in so-called charity today," he wrote, "it is probable that $950 is unwisely spent; so spent, indeed, as to produce the very evils which it proposes to mitigate or cure." "The amassing of wealth," he wrote elsewhere, "is one of the worst species of idolatry; no idol more debasing."

It is in the redemption of these promises that Carnegie's truest distinction lies. Before his life ended he had given away $324,657,399 — his secretary's exact figure — keeping only about $25 million. The manner in which he had given it, moreover, set a standard which the keepers of other fortunes, accidental or earned, had to try to equal.

In America, Britain, and Australia the name Carnegie is synonymous with "library." Properly speaking, he did not give libraries; he gave buildings, some 2,800 of them, which the various communities were expected to fill with books. His Universities Trust for the Scottish universities expressed an old loyalty, just as his special gifts to Pittsburgh — notably the Carnegie Institute, a combined library, art gallery, museum, and technical school — expressed a newer attachment. His Hero Funds carried into civilian life the recognition that military men received from the Victoria Cross and Congressional Medal. His Foundation for the Advancement of Teaching and his Endowment for International Peace have long promoted two great causes.

"The way of the philanthropist is hard," Carnegie wrote Rockefeller in 1911. He found that year that after all his gifts, he still had more than $150 million to dispense. His answer to the problem was the creation of the most massive of all his benefactions, the Carnegie Corporation of New York. To it while still active he transferred $125 million, and with augmented resources it still continues its many-sided usefulness. . . .

And what was the effect of all this proof that private fortunes are best treated, in Henry Ford's phrase, as reservoirs of public wealth? It is impossible to measure, but we may safely say that it has been profound. Abram S. Hewitt partially defined it. "Your example and your practise," he wrote Carnegie in 1901, "have provoked general discussion, and it is interesting to see that the duty of wealth announced in your book *The Gospel of Wealth* is now generally recognized by public opinion. The change is extraordinary, and before the century expires I expect society will see a very different state of feeling from that which now prevails, when class is arrayed against class. . . . It seems to me that your position in the history of social development will be that of the man who first compelled wealth to recognize its duties, not merely as a matter of moral obligation, but of a decent self-respect on the part of men who control large fortunes."

ALLAN NEVINS

Oregon's Crater Lake National Park, established during Roosevelt's Administration.

Photograph by Robert N. Taylor

PRESERVING THE NATURAL WEALTH

In this era of affluence, and of wide margins to life in increased mobility and leisure, one of Theodore Roosevelt's fighting achievements — in the eyes of himself and others his greatest achievement — ought to have a special appeal to all who believe in a beautiful America for our children and grandchildren. This was his battle for conservation; his fight against men like Joe Cannon, who banged his Speaker's desk shouting, "Not one cent for scenery!"

Roosevelt wanted a heroic America, and was heroic himself in battling crooked political bosses, special interests in finance and industry and exploiters of women, children and minority groups. But he wanted more than a heroic country; he wished a country with its natural resources left valuable for posterity. He demanded, as he put it, "the preservation of the

scenery, of the forests, of the wilderness life and the wilderness game for the people as a whole, instead of leaving the enjoyment thereof to be confined to the very rich who can control private reserves." He knew that unborn generations would need all the minerals, timber, water power and soil fertility that could be maintained for them. It was for a greener, more productive and more attractive America that he fought greedy lumbering, mining and ranching interests, blind Western governors and "the honest men of ultraconservative type who always dread change, whether good or bad."

What he did in this field, with Senator Francis G. Newlands of Nevada and Gifford Pinchot to aid him, is his most enduring monument, an object lesson to his successors.

When T.R. became President, out of

800,000,000 acres of virgin forest originally found on our 3,000,000 square miles, roughly 600,000,000 were gone; only a quarter of this vast woodland area remained. Though much of the clearance had been healthful, it was imperative to protect the remainder. Shortsighted owners would lay it waste as soon as dollars beckoned. In his first annual message Roosevelt declared: "The forest and water problems are perhaps the most vital internal questions of the United States." His initial step was to throw his weight behind an irrigation and reclamation bill sponsored by Senator Newlands and stymied in Congress. One result was its early passage, creating a reclamation service and setting aside proceeds from the sale of public lands for irrigating arid tracts. Before he left the White House, T.R. had started or finished about 30 irrigation projects, one of them including the Roosevelt Dam in Arizona. A larger result was that Roosevelt won the support of some previously chilly Western leaders.

Then he boldly took up the forestry situation. The statute books held a law of 1891 authorizing the President to set aside suitable areas as forest reserves. Grover Cleveland, a conservationist, had made use of it, but William McKinley had neglected it. Roosevelt, backed by a Public Land Commission appointed in 1903, invoked it in such sweeping fashion that by the end of his second term he had placed almost 150,000,000 acres in the reserves. In addition, at the suggestion of Senator Robert La Follette, he set aside 85,000 acres in Alaska and the Northwest until an exploration of their mineral resources could be made.

To crown his work for keeping America green, fertile and beautiful, Roosevelt, in May 1908, opened a Conservation Conference in the White House, to which he had invited all the governors, cabinet officers and Supreme Court justices, with such notable citizens as John

Theodore Roosevelt wanted a country heroic enough to preserve the wilderness for all the people.

In contrast to Theodore Roosevelt's trophy rooms at Sagamore Hill, New York, Mrs. Roosevelt's drawing room features damask textures and a pastel portrait of her.

Burroughs, Andrew Carnegie and James J. Hill. A great deal of truth lay in his subsequent boast. "It is doubtful," he wrote, "whether, except in time of war, any new idea of like importance has ever been presented to a nation and accepted by it with such effectiveness and rapidity as was the case with this conservation movement when it was introduced to the American people by the Conference. . . ." The delegates signed a unanimous declaration that the sources of national wealth exist for the people and should be guarded by all states. Forty-one states shortly established conservation commissions. Roosevelt meanwhile appointed a National Conservation Commission to assist and coordinate the work of the state bodies, and to prepare a three-volume report that proved a veritable Domesday Book in its full listing of natural wealth. Its chairman was Gifford Pinchot, who kept on fighting after T.R. left office.

Theodore Roosevelt's conservation has preserved today's beautiful things in a legacy for tomorrow's people.

All this is so impressive a story that we may almost agree with President Charles R. Van Hise of the University of Wisconsin that Roosevelt's conservation work stamped him as "one of the greatest statesmen of any nation of any time." People who use the five national parks he established, including Crater Lake in Oregon and Mesa Verde in Colorado, or his 16 national monuments, such as Mt. Olympus in Washington State and Muir Woods in California, will hardly dissent. One illustration of his boldness might well be taken to heart by other Presidents. When informed that extermination threatened the birds on a teeming island, he did not ask, "Is there a law authorizing me to act?" He asked, "Is there a law which forbids me to declare Pelican Island a Federal bird reservation?" — and on being told there was none, replied, "Very well, then I do declare it."

But his work for forest, mountain and river, and for appreciation of natural beauty and wildlife, by no means ended with legislation and executive orders. He lent his robust pen to the cause. In a long series of essays and books he extolled the permanent importance of central Colorado, western Montana and the Canadian Rockies (among other areas) as health resorts and playgrounds for the whole Union. In *Hunting Trips of a Ranchman* he made even the Bad Lands of Dakota seem fascinating. He knew birds as well as he knew politics; his first printed papers were on the birds of Oyster Bay and the Adirondacks. He took up ranching not so much because he hoped to make money from it (he lost) as because he exulted in the life, "its abounding vigor and its bold, restless freedom"; and he made the wild plains as attractive as the great tracts of primeval forest. His zest for the rifle rendered him familiar with all the fauna of the West: the cougars, lynxes, timber wolves, coyotes, bears, pronghorn antelope and bison. Few have written more expertly on those noble game animals, the elk, the mule deer and the mountain goat. Few have dealt more enthusiastically with scenic delights ranging from the Yellowstone Falls to Tensas Bayou in the Louisiana canebrakes.

The natural wealth of America will remain ours only if we fight, as Theodore Roosevelt fought, to keep it and enlarge it. We can find the joy of living with our heritage of desert sunsets, cliff-walled canyons, mighty redwoods, murmuring white pine forests, inland seas, and rockbound coasts only if we have Roosevelt's ardor — fortified by science — for the wild.

ALLAN NEVINS

A NATION SHAPED by ITS DAILY CRAFTS

Folk arts and crafts — at once utilitarian and decorative — are evidence of a time when citizens found delight in making everyday things both clever and functional.

The American eagle is a ubiquitous motif in the nation's folk art and was often used as a figurehead on ships. This small eagle is at rest, but similar figures were carved much larger and poised for flight. The scrollwork under its talons is typical of bow decorations on sailing ships.

Eagle, carved figurehead. The Mariners Museum, Newport News, Virginia

Scrimshaw etchings, done by whalers during idle time, were designs carved, pricked or scraped in outline on the whalebone. Sometimes whalemen used a picture from a book or magazine as guide. The engraving process that followed was more delicate, and fine inking or coloring distinguished the more ambitious artisans.

Sighting Whales, scrimshaw. The Mariners Museum, Newport News, Virginia

Pennsylvania blanket and
dower chests like this poplar
piece from Lebanon County
(circa 1800) were traditionally
painted warm red, blue, green or yellow,
with two or three front panels designed with
stylized flowers, urns, pillars and arches.

Pennsylvania German chest. The Henry Ford Museum, Dearborn, Michigan

Opposite:
New Englanders also enjoyed painted country furniture, but in more subdued reds and greens. These shades enhance the Fitch House kitchen where eighteenth-century cookery is displayed on a red highboy and chest.

Fitch House kitchen. Old Sturbridge Village, Massachusetts

The four-poster, spool-turned bed remained popular during the nineteenth century. This particular piece has interchangeable posters: Tall ones support the tester in winter, and short ones bring the mosquito netting closer in summer.

Spool-turned bed. Jean Baptiste Vallé House, Ste. Genevieve, Missouri.

Pewter (tin alloyed with copper) was commonly used for all those utensils for which we now use ceramics, steel and aluminum. American pewterers worked predominantly between 1700 and 1850, crafting objects like the covered tankard, a rare piece in American homes and taverns.

American pewter. The Adam Thoroughgood House, Norfolk, Virginia

TIME OF DECISION

Nature endows our country with an abundance, and our citizens despoil nature of its beauty and order. Our country preserves the inherent rights of its citizens, and its citizens exploit their fellowmen. What wisdom is there in violence, and what gain in greed? From where will come the power to heal, and who shall bring the strength to endure?

THE DELIBERATE CITY

The city was never a deliberate thing. It never really happened by design; forever it has resulted from a convergence of necessities. In the earliest days the necessity was protection: You walled a city, fortified the wall and kept out invaders or robbers or barbarians. The came the industrial revolution, and the city was a labor pool and a center of transportation facilities to bring in raw material and ship out finished goods. Circumstances, not the urge to create a place for living, spawned cities. Any planning that was done was mechanical — laying out symmetrical street patterns or designing buildings — often more to meet economic requirements than the needs and desires of human beings.

The bookkeeping of urban redevelopment as it is practiced generally is understandable, but it becomes more complicated as the human factors creep in and begin to elbow out the statistics and rates of interest and depreciation calculations.

But these human factors must creep in. Cities are for living in. They are for people. Deep in their hearts, people recognize this, and will come back willingly and cheerfully when cities begin to adjust to the lives of their citizens with more thoroughness than is apparent anywhere at this writing. What is needed now is a concerted effort to orient "redevelopment" toward people instead of toward economics — and if this is done, the economics, over the years, will take care of itself. It will take thinking, hoping, feeling and experimenting. It will not be easy. There will be opposition and impatience and disbelief. But it certainly will be done.

Cities will become more deliberate things. For the first time in all history, they will begin to shape themselves to spiritual and human requirements, and the architect and the contractor and the tax collector and the bookkeeper will learn to cut the cloth to fit the pattern. The deliberate city of the future is the one that starts at the neighborhood level and moves in all directions. It starts with the emotion of city living and builds the mechanics to suit. It starts with people. It ends with people. It is people.

FRED SMITH

Where redevelopment tears down the city of necessity, there is hope of building a city for people.

AIR POLLUTION'S DESTRUCTIVENESS

Air pollution can no longer be taken lightly. Scientists have recently accumulated a mass of evidence that indicates that air-borne contaminants can trigger bronchitis and other respiratory illnesses; that hydrocarbons from vehicle exhaust fumes and petroleum refineries are capable of causing lung cancer; that other pollutants can disintegrate nylon stockings, crumble marble, and turn white houses black overnight. . . .

Lately, officials with a concern for our national food resources have cast an anxious eye toward the farms. What effect, they asked, does industrial waste in the air have on crops and livestock? To what extent have our factories usurped the property rights of our farm owners?

The answers are not hard to find: **In Florida,** contamination from phosphate factories has injured cattle to such an extent that ranching is no longer profitable in the affected areas. **In New Jersey**, Rutgers University plant pathologists discovered ozone is threatening the continued production of spinach and endive.

These episodes are typical of what is happening today across the nation. As our exploding metropolises push outward, long-established farming enterprises are drowning in an ocean of poisonous air. Never before has man fashioned so great and devastating a change in his own environment.

In addition to these portents of doom, some farmers insist the unabated flow of foul air across their land is an affront to their status as citizens. Has a property right been taken from the farmer as a result of the pollution of air over his land?

Charles Butler of the American Farm Bureau Federation tackled this question in 1958 at the National Conference on Air Pollution. His conclusion was positive: Contaminated air does, indeed, usurp the established farmer's property

With rapid city and industrial expansion, America has a critical shortage of clean, fresh air.

U.S. Public Health Service

rights. "This being the case," said Butler, "the farmer should be paid just compensation for damages to his enterprise."

In many areas, industrialists have been paying farm owners astronomical sums in compensation for loss and injury of crops resulting from air pollution. Most farmers, however, must look to the courts for satisfaction. But here again they run the risk of disenchantment, for they feel from long experience that too often courts and juries are guided in their decisions by the manufacturer's more impressive contribution to the community in terms of employment and tax dollars. Few men who work the soil, however, are inclined to grow plants for the purpose of filing claims or soliciting pay-offs. . . .

Already there are, according to a Public Health Service count, six thousand communities across the nation that have air pollution problems of varying degrees. Most of these cities and towns lie clustered within the great metropolitan areas — the super-cities. Collectively they cover less than ten percent of the nation's land area, yet one out of every two Americans lives somewhere within their illdefined boundaries.

The super-city also harbors the overwhelming majority of the country's automobile crankcases, incinerators, chimneys, furnaces, and factories — all the large and small contributors to our polluted skies. And here, too, in the belts of green between the super-city's member communities, are the postage-stamp farms and dairies that provide the bulk of fresh produce available to every second American at his neighborhood super market.

Urban-fringe farmers stand today upon a vanishing agricultural frontier. The belts of green are getting thinner and thinner. The expressways and housing developments are slicing through their land. When toxic irritants descend from the sky, it is the cell of the growing plant that dies first. Air pollution can do to the farmer what no expressway or subdivision could ever do: It can destroy living things before his very eyes. It can destroy his spirit.

JOHN G. MITCHELL

U.S. Department of the Interior Conservation Yearbook and Fuller Co.

Left and opposite: Both man-made and natural monuments are defaced by civilization's smog.

WATER POLLUTION CRISIS

For at least half a century, this country has neglected one of its most precious natural resources. It has permitted its cities, farms, and industries to dump wastes into its rivers and streams in many cases without plan, without controls, and without particular thought.

It is not difficult to indict water pollution. It is an economic burden which is robbing us of water we need. It is a menace to health and in many communities an aesthetic horror; it is also a destroyer of fish and wildlife habitat. Yet it need not exist. Serious pollution can be prevented in most bodies of water and where it cannot be prevented, it can be controlled.

The reason for our failure to do this is partly public opinion. Of all our public works projects, waste treatment facilities are the least glamorous, the hardest to sell. Schools, highways, parks, playgrounds, and hospitals — all these have usually had precedence in public financing. At the same time, law enforcement has sometimes flagged in the face of public apathy, or when it has encountered a strong, well-financed opposition, or when public funds have been inadequate for thorough investigation and prosecution. . . .

More than a quarter of our cities today still discharge their wastes into the nearest stream without any treatment at all. Another thirty per cent provide only "primary" treatment, which utilizes screens and settling tanks to remove solids, a technique which at best removes thirty-five per cent of the organic wastes. The most efficient conventional plants, using "secondary" treatment, rely on bacterial action to eat up dissolved organic matter. This removes up to ninety per cent of this material although it leaves untouched many other kinds of pollutants.

Adding to the problem in many parts of America are our hastily built "septic tank suburbias." Too often these unsewered communities are developed without proper unit spacing of homes — or worse, on impervious soils which cannot adequately filter the wastes. As a result, home disposal units drain into the aquifer to contaminate underground water supplies, or seep up and spill over into surface water.

It will cost $600 million annually for the next ten years to bring our municipal sewage treatment facilities up-to-date and to take care of growing population and industry. At the same time it will cost another $600 million annually in industry expenditures if our factories are also to keep pace. . . .

This is one-half the problem: to build new treatment facilities. The other half of the problem is to develop more efficient techniques of water treatment. Today's methods of treating waste have hardly changed over the past fifty years; they are effective only in breaking down organic materials.

Research is obviously necessary, research to find new ways of removing material from water and for recovering and perhaps even utilizing chemical wastes. Many such studies are under way by the Federal Government, industry, universities, and various research agencies.

Fundamentally, no change of any moment takes place in our country unless there is first a public opinion that wants such a change. One of the elements which must go into water pollution control is public money. This is forthcoming when citizens are willing to work for it. A second thing needed in the water pollution field is better financed and better supported local, state, and interstate control agencies. A third requirement for water pollution abatement is the willingness to approach pollution on a river basin level. Water is no respecter of state or even national lines; it simply flows downhill. This is why what Chicago does in Lake Michigan is of concern not only to Chicago and to Illinois but to all our Lake States and to Canada. This is why we need interstate agencies and why comprehensive river basin water pollution control programs are a very important part of our Federal control program.

There is obviously work to be done by the citizens. We are the ones who complain about the funny taste in our drinking water, the bathing beaches posted as unsafe, the fifteen million fish which were killed last year by pollution, the ugly and smelly state of our rivers and streams. And it is we and our children who must sometime pay the piper for polluted water unless something is done about it now.

G. E. McCallum

The struggle for a clean drink of water emphasizes the urgency for pollution prevention and control.

SCENIC HIGHWAYS

It is not a matter of junk yards versus beauty or of outdoor advertising versus stagnation of commerce. With proper regulation and cooperation, we can have both — the junk yards and the billboards — without unduly sacrificing either the beauty of the landscape or the health of our economy. It is a matter of finding out how we can make those who "couldn't care less" care a little bit more. . . .

It is just as true in a crowded metropolis as it is in a National Park. Beauty begets beauty. We cannot, therefore, afford to limit our interests to anything less than the entire American land-

scape. We are judged as a nation on how we treat the land we live on, whether it is privately or publicly owned.

Park development programs in connection with the Interstate Highway System already have considerable leeway for landscaping work — including the construction of scenic overlooks, picnic areas, roadside parks and other amenities to make driving a pleasure. Unfortunately, this authority is scarcely being utilized at all. It is my hope that in the near future the coordinated effort needed for this park and landscape work can be brought about through closer cooperation with local, state and national programs.

Modern, uncluttered, scenic interstate highways can help citizens to experience the natural beauty of the American landscape.

To me, a scenic highway or parkway is, in effect, an elongated park. It should give the motorist generally the same kind of enjoyment which a pedestrian might expect from a walk through groves or gardens. The experience should be scenic, leisurely, refreshing and as relaxed as a motorist's responsibilities can permit. This is what we strive for in our National Parks and Parkways; this is what we encourage in the development of other roads and highways throughout the United States. From my talks with high officials of the Bureau of Public Roads I know they are taking this problem to heart and are making efforts to improve the present condition.

As a professional park man, I have tried, in my trips across the country, to visualize how America will look fifty years from now when most of our land patterns will have become permanently fixed. I am constantly reminded that in spite of the increasing success of our conservation programs there is much to be done and little time in which to do it. . . .

This is a fruitful country — a prosperous country — and the demands of a growing industrial society are constantly challenging the last remaining natural hillsides, fields and forests. We cannot expect to hold back the growing tide of progress, nor would we wish to do so. It is this very progress that provides a healthy

From the flower box to parks and seashores, keeping America beautiful
is increasingly being accepted as an individual and social responsibility.

B. C. Prentice

economy — progress which means more spendable, income, more leisure time for worthy pursuits and greater mobility to get to new places of scenic, scientific or historic importance. But we can work with progress to guide it along the road to a realization of long range economic and cultural values.

The challenge is twofold: to develop in the hearts of all Americans a deep awareness of conservation and love of our natural and historic heritage; and to provide, in response to the recreation demands of an ever-increasing population, more park and recreation resources at the municipal, state and Federal levels to meet adequately our present and future needs.

President John F. Kennedy expressed this when he said: "I don't think there is anything that could occupy our attention with more distinction than trying to preserve for those who come after us this beautiful country which we have inherited."

Keeping America beautiful starts with the flower box; it continues through clean, well-kept neighborhoods with city parks and playgrounds; it is reflected in the self-respect of commercial and industrial establishments proud of their public image. And along our highways and parkways, we emerge from the manicured lawns and shrubs to the wide natural vistas of beautiful open country, to broad recreation areas, to the scenic wonders of our National Parks, to the vast reaches of our National Seashores, to the deep woods of our National Forests and into the wild primeval wilderness areas, where man is only a visitor and nature is supreme.

To accomplish this master plan for America it will take the continued cooperative efforts of every civic and governmental group — national, state and local. It will take the sound administration of agencies such as the National Park Service, the Bureau of Outdoor Recreation, the Fish and Wildlife Service, the National Forest Service, the Bureau of Public Roads, the Corps of Engineers. And it will take the most enlightened coordination of the nation's conservation leadership — embodied as it is in such large part in the Department of the Interior — to bring a new order to our natural wonders and to assure the American people of an orderly and beautiful country with adequate park and recreation opportunities now and for generations to come.

CONRAD L. WIRTH

DEATH OF A TREE

Somehow, the destruction of a tree diminishes me, and, in a wider sense, all of us. The invention of the power saw has wrought havoc in many places; it is always so much easier for the average man to cut down a tree that has taken many decades to grow than to plant another and wait upon its growing, though the individual man is not as often guilty of this attitude as are governmental bodies. Village, town, country, even state government commissions and departmental bodies — with the insistence of so many highway department officials on straight roads, free of growth on the tree banks for twenty to forty feet back from the roadway — are thus doing an incalculable amount of damage to the beauty of the countryside and contributing to a distortion of its normal ecology.

I think well of any man who takes care of his trees; I agree with Thoreau that large old trees about a house are "a surer indication of old family distinction and worth than any evidence of wealth" and that evidence of "care bestowed on these trees secures the traveler's respect as for a nobler husbandry than the raising of corn and potatoes." And by the same token I am inclined to think less well of those who are careless of their trees — owners of wood lots who permit logging at great damage to all uncut trees and with wood lots left uncleaned, those landholders who top their trees for any other reason but an attempt to save them from infection spreading through the trees. Many a fine old piece of property has been despoiled by insensitive new owners who feel compelled to lay ax or saw to the very assets which lend property its distinction. I count such men poor shoats indeed, beset by limitations of insensitivity and lack of aesthetic appreciation of such a nature as to tend to make them undesirable company.

Any piece of land is the more valuable if there are trees on it, and any settlement of men is incomplete without trees to lend their character and beauty to it. Man's awareness of natural beauty is slow to come in a civilization that holds up material success as the ideal goal — yet it must surely be latent in all men.

A man who can walk in a grove of hard maple

Robert N. Taylor

Trees which have taken dozens of years to attain maturity can be destroyed in a few minutes by modern machinery.

Gordon and Jeanne Chambers

Trees lend character and beauty to any settlement of man.

trees on a cloudy day, when the trees are so yellow with leaves that their glow is caught and held in the very air as if the sun were shining there — who can cross a birch-dotted slope on a day in April when the wind bends the white boles and makes the yellow catkins dance on the blue heaven — who can hike through the marshes and meadows on a wintry February day when the upthrusting sap has given new colors to the lowland in the brightened mustard of willows, the maroon of alders, the red of osiers and the first gray pussy willow catkins are breaking their sheaths — who can wander in a sugarbush with the moonlight glinting on the buckets hung about the trees and the night aromatic with the elusive fragrance of sap dripping musically from the tapped trunks — and not be lifted up, however briefly, out of his mundane world, his soul restored, is dead to beauty and the experience of beauty indeed.

AUGUST DERLETH

AMERICA at WORK and LEISURE

Through the years artists and authors have depicted our people in the activities of everyday life and have captured the diverse spirit of the American community.

For a long time [Rip Van Winkle] used to console himself, when driven from home, by frequenting a kind of perpetual club of sages, philosophers, and other idle personages of the village; which held its sessions on a bench before a small inn. . . .
The opinions of this junto were completely controlled by Nicholas Vedder, a patriarch of the village, and landlord of the inn. . . .

Washington Irving (1783-1859) From **Rip Van Winkle**

Rip Van Winkle At Nicholas Vedder's Tavern by John Quidor (1801-1881). Courtesy Museum of Fine Arts, Boston

The face of the night, the heart of the dark, the tongue of the flame—I had known all things that lived or stirred or worked below her destiny. I was the child of night, a son among her mighty family, and I knew all that moved within the hearts of men who loved the night.

Thomas Wolfe (1900-1938) From **Death the Proud Brother**

Excerpt from "Death the Proud Brother" (copyright 1933 Charles Scribner's Sons; renewal copyright©1961 Pincus Berner) is reprinted with the permission of Charles Scribner's Sons from *From Death to Morning* by Thomas Wolfe.

Nighthawks by Edward Hopper (1882-   ). Oil. Courtesy of The Art Institute of Chicago, Friends of American Art Collection

Rushing along on a narrow reach,
  Our rival under the lee,
The wind falls foul of the weather leach,
  And the jib flaps fretfully.

Thomas Fleming Day (1861-1927) From **The Main-Sheet Song**

Excerpt from "The Main-Sheet Song" by Thomas Fleming Day. Courtesy of Rudder Magazine, June, 1965.

Yacht Race by Maurice Prendergast (1859-1924). Water color. Courtesy of The Art Institute of Chicago, Watson F. Blair purchase prize

Aiding A Comrade by Frederic Remington (1861-1909). Oil. Hogg Brothers Collection, The Museum of Fine Arts, Houston

Cowboy, cattleman, cowpuncher, it matters not what name others have given him, he has remained—himself . . . . He never dreamed he was a hero.

Emerson Hough (1857-1923) From **The Story of the Cowboy**

The sun up-sprang,
Its light swept the plain like a sea
Of golden water, and the blue-gray dome
That soared above the settler's shack
Was lighted into magical splendor.

Hamlin Garland (1860-1940) From **Prairie Songs**

The Homestead by John Steuart Curry (1897-1946). Mural. Courtesy of U.S. Department of the Interior

Twelve o'clock. There went up a roar that drowned the crack of the soldiers' musketry as they fired in the air as the signal of noon and the start of the Run. . . . The thousands surged over the Line. It was like water going over a broken dam. The rush had started, and it was devil take the hindmost. We swept across the prairie in a cloud of black and red dust. . . .

Edna Ferber (1887-   ) From **Cimarron**

Excerpt from *Cimarron*. Copyright 1929, 1930 by Edna Ferber. Reprinted with permission.

Oklahoma Land Rush by John Steuart Curry (1897-1946). Mural. Courtesy of U.S. Department of the Interior

V
IN SEARCH
OF EXCELLENCE
IN DIVERSITY

A measure and a moment meet to make a man. Whatever inspires the mind, strengthens the will, and ennobles love, that is birth. When time demands a change and destiny challenges the greatness of man, that is growth. When man can return in responsible stewardship what he has received as endowed gifts, that is maturity.

NEED FOR IMAGINATION

Not only to prevent an unnecessary waste of happiness in our people, not only to prevent the breeding of thoughtless monsters, not only to realize fully the urgency of the situation of the underprivileged nations, not only to develop the arts do we so badly need to develop our imagination. We need it too in order to tackle one of the main tasks of our time — the reconciliation of modern man with his surroundings. Ludwig Erhard, former West German minister of economics, stated recently that man feels a deep bewilderment and discontent with his surroundings today. Such bewilderment shows itself, for instance, in the movement of people to the suburbs, although they may feel most at home in cities, and in the cynical way that many modern writers describe the role of nature in our world. . . .

We have proven once again in our time the old truth that wealth does not make people happy. The achievement of a higher living standard in foreign countries and the preservation of wealth on our North American continent should be a beginning, not a guiding idea. We have to find a new, more appreciative conception of nature and all creation. We have to change our cities, suburbs and farms to make them into more adequate surroundings for a changed modern man and we have to teach man to master spiritually a changed world. To accomplish this we have to develop a more acute imagination to enable us to come to realize the potentials around us and within us and thus gather the strength to make the world a better place in which to live.

FRANCES SYDOW

Opposite: By serving abroad, in programs such as the Peace Corps, Americans will develop a more acute imagination to realize their potential.

CONSIDER OUR ABUNDANCE

The wheat will not have fulfilled its destiny until it has traveled far, has changed owners a few times, and, finally, has satisfied an appetite.

At late harvest time in 1960, the U.S.A.'s 1961 wheat crop was estimated at 1,204,000,000 bushels. If all of it were made into bread and divided equally among our 183,000,000 population, every American could have a whole loaf every day for a year — and 75 loaves to spare!

What is remarkable about this? In this land of plenty, there is always wheat for enough bread — all we can eat, all we can sell abroad, some to give away in year-round Christmas charity, and plenty for reserve.

But it is remarkable. Whether looking back over the dead centuries or across today's living hemispheres, abundance is seen as a rarity, and scarcity as commonplace. There have always been more hungry human beings than ones with enough to eat. This is true even today.

Perhaps, it is time to consider our abundances — even in the form of a loaf of bread, the commercial manna.

WHEELER MCMILLEN

Opposite: In America there is wheat for enough bread.
Above: America's farmland produces an abundance of food.

Shostal

Workers achieve art when their labor is touched by love and pride.

ART IN WORK

Industrial workers are often pictured in dank, grease-saturated plants or in dry, antiseptic, windowless ones. Obviously both of these scenes are quite far from the country beautiful. But there are others. For instance, the welders in the above picture have a backdrop equal to that of a forest ranger, a sheepherder or a man of the sea.

Perhaps these workers in this setting have come close to attaining what Joseph Conrad once described:

"Efficiency of a practically flawless kind may be reached naturally in the struggle for bread. But there is something beyond — a higher point, a subtle and unmistakable touch of love and pride beyond mere skill; almost an inspiration which gives to all work that finish which is almost art — which *is* art."

CARL SANDBURG'S "CONNEMARA"

I must confess that I am no scenery man. I am always talking, always interested in the conversation with the result that the River Rhine looked much like North Carolina's Catawba to me. I am, however, willing to pay the price. If I don't see all there is to see, still I get to hear all there is to hear.

The one American scene that stops me talking, however, is the view from Carl Sandburg's front porch in Flat Rock, North Carolina. The Sandburg farm is called "Connemara" and it is an extensive piece of land. The house is mounted on the crest of a wooded hill and from the top of the steps to their front door a man can see the land stretch down, smooth as silk, to the lake below and from the lake roll away for miles in every direction into the Sapphire Hills of the Great Smoky Mountains. Even on a cloudy day Mt. Mitchell is visible.

The first time I looked upon this breath-taking scene from the porch of the antebellum mansion, I faced Sandburg and said, "Your old Socialist colleagues up in Wisconsin must be turning over in their graves."

HARRY GOLDEN

Carl Sandburg's "Connemara" in Flat Rock, North Carolina. Extensive natural beauty surrounds the antebellum mansion of America's great poet.

81

Dispossessed plantation house.

FAULKNER'S MISSISSIPPI

The rich deep black alluvial soil which would grow cotton taller than the head of a man on a horse, already one jungle one brake one impassable density of brier and cane and vine interlocking the soar of gum and cypress and hickory and pinoak and ash, printed now by the tracks of unalien shapes — bear and deer and panthers and bison and wolves and alligators and the myriad smaller beasts, and unalien men to name them too perhaps — the (themselves) nameless though recorded predecessors who built the mounds to escape the spring floods and left their meagre artifacts: the obsolete and the dispossessed, dispossessed by those who were dispossessed in turn because they too were obsolete: the wild Algonquian, Chickasaw and Choctaw and Natchez and Pascagoula, peering in virgin astonishment down from the tall bluffs at a Chippeway canoe bearing three Frenchmen — and had barely time to whirl and look behind him at ten and then a hundred and then a thousand Spaniards come overland from the Atlantic Ocean: a tide, a wash, a thrice flux-and-ebb of motion so rapid and quick across the land's slow alluvial chronicle as to resemble the limber flicking of the magician's one hand before the other holding the deck of inconstant cards: the Frenchman for a moment, then the Spaniard for perhaps two, then the Frenchman for another two and then the Spaniard again for another and then the Frenchman for that one last second, half-breath; because then came the Anglo-Saxon, the pioneer, the tall man, roaring with Protestant scripture and boiled whisky, Bible and jug in one hand and (like as not) a native tomahawk in the other, brawling, turbulent not through viciousness but simply because of his over-revved glands; uxorious and polygamous: a married invincible bachelor, dragging his gravid wife and most of the rest of his mother-in-law's family behind him into the trackless infested forest, spawning that child as like as not behind the barricade of a rifle-crotched log mapless leagues from nowhere and then getting her with another one before reaching his final itch-footed destination, and at the same time scattering his ebullient seed in a hundred dusky bellies through a thousand miles of wilderness; innocent and gullible, without bowels for avarice or compassion or forethought either, changing the face of the earth: felling a tree which took two hundred years to grow, in order to extract from it a bear or a capful of wild honey.

Obsolete too: still felling the two-hundred-year-old tree when the bear and the wild honey were gone and there was nothing in it any more but a raccoon or a possum whose hide was

Portico: the tomorrowless days are gone.

Above: Haunts along the Natchez trace.

Right: Fishing boat at Biloxi.

worth at the most two dollars, turning the earth into a howling waste from which he would be the first to vanish, not even on the heels but synchronous with the slightly darker wild men whom he had dispossessed, because, like them, only the wilderness could feed and nourish him; and so disappeared, strutted his roaring eupeptic hour, and was no more, leaving his ghost, pariah and proscribed, scriptureless now and armed only with the highwayman's, the murderer's, pistol, haunting the fringes of the wilderness which he himself had helped to destroy, because the river towns marched now recessional south by south along the processional bluffs: St. Louis, Paducah, Memphis, Helena, Vicksburg, Natchez, Baton Rouge, peopled by men with mouths full of law, in broadcloth and flowered waistcoats, who owned Negro slaves and Empire beds and buhl cabinets and ormolu clocks, who strolled and smoked their cigars along the bluffs beneath which in the shanty and flatboat purlieus he rioted out the last of his doomed evening, losing his worthless life again and again to the fierce knives of his drunken and worthless kind — this in the intervals of being pursued and harried in his vanishing avatars of Harpe and Hare and Mason and Murrel, either shot on sight or hoicked, dragged out of what remained of his secret wilderness haunts along the overland Natchez trace (one day someone brought a curious seed into the land and inserted it into the earth, and now vast fields of white not only covered the waste places which with his wanton and heedless axe he had made, but were effacing, thrusting back the wilderness even faster than he had been able to, so that he barely had a screen for his back when, crouched in his thicket, he glared at his dispossessor in impotent and incredulous and uncomprehending rage) into the towns to his formal apotheosis in a courtroom and then a gallows or the limb of a tree;

Because those days were gone, the old brave innocent tumultuous eupeptic tomorrowless days; the last broadhorn and keelboat (Mike Fink was a legend; soon even the grandfathers would no longer claim to remember him, and the river hero was now the steamboat gambler wading ashore in his draggled finery from the towhead where the captain had marooned him) had been sold piecemeal for firewood in Chartres and Toulouse and Dauphine street, and Choctaw and Chickasaw braves, in short hair and overalls and armed with mule-whips in place of war-clubs and already packed up to move west to Oklahoma, watched steamboats furrowing even the shallowest and remotest wilderness streams where tumbled gently to the motion of the paddle-wheels, the gutted rock-weighted bones of Hare's and Mason's murderees; a new time, a new age, millennium's beginning; one vast single net of commerce webbed and veined the midcontinent's fluvial embracement; New Orleans, Pittsburgh, and Fort Bridger, Wyoming, were suburbs one to the other, inextricable in destiny; men's mouths were full of law and order, all men's mouths were round with the sound of money; one unanimous golden affirmation ululated the nation's boundless immeasurable forenoon: profit plus regimen equals security: a nation of commonwealths; that crumb, that dome, that gilded pustule, that Idea risen now, suspended like a balloon or a portent or a thundercloud above what used to be wilderness, drawing, holding the eyes of all: Mississippi.

WILLIAM FAULKNER

HOUSES OF WORSHIP

No matter what the nation's perhaps over-abundant materialistic distractions may be, America is still a nation of churchgoers. In this country one just cannot escape the appeal and traditions of the houses of God. They are constantly before our eyes — in teeming cities, in quiet villages, at the confluence of deserts and mountains, and still clanging their bells as the fishing boats sail home to ports like Gloucester, Massachusetts, and San Francisco, California.

Not all churches are great edifices, and the test of American religious faith is that the same humbling-before-God exists in the austere Quaker meeting house in the hills of Pennsylvania, the white clapboard Protestant church among the cornfields of Iowa or on the plains of South Dakota, the mammoth arena where evangelist Billy Graham holds meetings and the humble Baptist Negro "shack" in the Deep South.

In the words of St. Paul: "Extinguish not the spirit" the American churches seem to tell all Americans eternally. These residuals of our eternal belief came from Europe, Asia and Africa. In such a richly endowed people it would seem impossible for our solemn and multifarious houses of God to be less than pre-eminent as our prevailing point of contact with a wise, merciful and just God.

A few years before his death, John Adams,

Above: St. James the Fisherman Episcopal Chapel, Cape Cod, designed by Olav Hammarstrom.

Opposite: Holy Hill, Discalced Carmelite monastery south of Hartford, Wisconsin.

one of the nation's Founding Fathers, wrote to an old friend: "A kind Providence has preserved and supported me for 85 years and seven months, through many dangers and difficulties . . . and I am not afraid to trust in its goodness to all eternity. . . . I am willing to await the order of the Supreme Power. We shall leave the world with many consolations. It is better than we found it. . . . Our Country has brilliant and exhilarating prospects before it. . . ."

America has been fortunate to have more than its share of citizens who believed and continue to believe as Adams did.

Joel Strasser

MODERN CHURCH ARCHITECTURE

Above: Salem Lutheran Church, Deerwood, Minnesota.
Built of native fieldstone and timber.

Little more than 35 years ago it was often difficult to distinguish a newly built church from an old one. Despite new needs, most designs followed the medieval cathedral as a basic model: The vaulted ceiling became in our time a plaster vault painted to simulate stone, and buttresses buttressed nothing. Modern church architecture uses fresh materials and forms, such as reinforced concrete, sheet copper, the folded slab, the spiral, and returns to stained glass and wood. Effective combination of these elements provides a place where living people worship.

Trappist Christmas pageant: Mirror is symbolic crib, candles represent Christ, "Light of the World."

GREAT MOMENTS, HISTORIC and SYMBOLIC

Painters have discerned singular impressions of historic and literary events which extend the vision of American poets and historians.

To him who in the love of Nature holds
Communion with her visible forms, she speaks
A various language; for his gayer hours
She has a voice of gladness, and a smile
And eloquence of beauty, and she glides
Into his darker musings, with a mild
And healing sympathy, that steals away
Their sharpness, ere he is aware.

William Cullen Bryant (1794-1878) From **Thanatopsis**

Kindred Spirits (William Cullen Bryant and Thomas Cole) by Asher Brown Durand (1796-1886). The New York Public Library. (Francis G. Mayer, N.Y.C.)

A hurry of hoofs in a village street,
A shape in the moonlight, a bulk in the dark,
And beneath, from the pebbles, in passing,
    a spark
Struck out by a steed flying fearless and
      fleet:
That was all! And yet, through the gloom
     and the light,
The fate of a nation was riding that
     night. . . .

Henry Wadsworth Longfellow (1807-1882) From **Paul Revere's Ride**

Midnight Ride of Paul Revere by Grant Wood (1892-1942). Metropolitan Museum of Art

Then we pursued the course of the stream for three miles, till it emptied into a river from the east. In the wide valley at their junction, we discovered a large camp of Indians. When we reached them and alighted from our horses we were received with great cordiality.

Meriwether Lewis (1774-1809) and **William Clark** (1770-1838) From
Journals of the Expedition

Lewis And Clark Meeting Flathead Indians by Charles M. Russell (1864-1926). Mural. Montana Historical Society

Fur Trappers Rendezvous by Alfred Jacob Miller
(1810-1874). (Wallace Kirkland)

Tent and tipis spread along the creeks. Large herds of horses and mules grazed the plain. Every day or so another little group came in, from as far away as the Three Forks, or South Park, or Brown's Hole. They had the winter's histories to exchange, the absent and the killed to account for, fellowship to renew.

Bernard De Voto (1897-1955) From **Across the Wide Missouri**